TRANSFORMING
COMMUNITY

TRANSFORMING COMMUNITY

THE WESLEYAN WAY
TO MISSIONAL CONGREGATIONS

HENRY H. KNIGHT III
F. DOUGLAS POWE, JR.

DISCIPLESHIP
RESOURCES

ISBNs
978-0-88177-754-3 (print)
978-0-88177-755-0 (mobi)
978-0-88177-756-7 (ePub)

Library of Congress Control Number: 2014952832

DR754

ACKNOWLEDGMENTS

We appreciate JillAnn Meunier editing the document and helping us to format it for publication. We also appreciate Rev. Jessica Anschutz and Rev. Paul Johnson for allowing us to use their work in the book.

CONTENTS

INTRODUCTION

In *Transforming Evangelism,* we attempted to help congregations to reclaim the "E" word from a Wesleyan perspective. We did this by focusing on the Wesleyan theme of loving God and neighbor. John and Charles Wesley believed that it is those who first have God's love in their hearts who then share that love with others. Their language for this was that holiness of heart leads to holiness of life. For early Methodists, their experiences of God's holy love and its making a home in their hearts infused them with desire to share the good news of Jesus Christ with others, and to meet the desperate physical and spiritual needs of people. As the scripture says, "We love because he first loved us" (1 John 4:19).

The Wesley brothers saw this transforming work of God occurring in community. Their Methodist movement consisted of an array of communities, each designed to welcome the work of God in its midst. Their goal was not only the transformation of persons but the renewal of the church and the wider society in holy love.

Today God continues to work in the world, sharing the love of Jesus Christ through the power of the Holy Spirit. God intends for Christian congregations and communities to be a part of this mission of God. But for a community to have a missional passion, it must first have a missional heart. And to have a missional heart, a community must itself be shaped by the love of Christ and be a place where persons are being shaped by that love.

This book presents a Wesleyan way to form missional communities and congregations. It is based on the conviction that just as holiness of heart leads to holiness of life, it is communities of holy love that actively participate in God's mission in the world.

If communities of holy love are foundational to missional congregations, how do we form such communities? In part 1, we show that communities of faith both shape and are shaped by key Christian practices such as worship, sacraments, studying the Bible, prayer, mutual care, and mutual accountability. These practices are not new. Many know from their own experiences how a Sunday school class, which has been together for thirty years and supported one another through life's ups and downs, has shaped their lives even as their lives have shaped that community. Intentional efforts are needed to strengthen existing practices while expanding to incorporate a broader array of practices.

Many Sunday school classes also know that over time new persons no longer join them. When visitors do come, they tend not to remain in the class. What has happened? Are those in the class no longer being shaped by the community, or are they shaping it in inhospitable ways of which they are unaware? We will draw on the Wesleyan tradition to provide insights on how to maintain the vitality of faith communities as centers of holy love.

If a community is shaped by the love of God in Jesus Christ, it cannot keep that love to itself. This was certainly true of early Methodists. John and Charles Wesley desired to transform the broader English society for Christ and did this by seeking to reach those persons not actively participating in the Church of England. They preached in the fields, visited those in prison, and fed the hungry. They and their followers initiated a range of ministries to address the needs of the desperately poor. They were out in the community making a difference in people's lives. And in the process, they were growing new communities as more and more turned to Christ.

The challenge facing many congregations today is similar: how can they make a difference in the broader community and do so in the name of Christ? Communities of holy love have the desire and motivation to participate in God's mission in the world, but are often limited in their vision of how to go about it. This is the concern of part 2.

The Wesleyan tradition understands God's mission to be holistic, concerned with both sharing our faith and addressing social ills in a range of ways. Today the tendency is to either seek to engage in social action or to share the gospel message. This schism confronts us in various forms: justice ministries versus proclamation, social gospel versus evangelism, and so on. The inability to see how a congregation can make a difference in the broader community while doing so in the name of Jesus is contributing to the decline of vital congregations in our day. We hope to provide insights on how to see the world through Wesleyan eyes, which will equip congregations to be transformational in a more holistic manner.

A theme running through this book is organizing community for formation of members and for mission in the world. John Wesley was able to transform faith communities and the broader community because he was a superb organizer. Today we use words like "entrepreneurial" to describe what is needed in ministry. While the word was unknown to Wesley, his ability to organize formational communities that enabled persons to increasingly have Christ-centered lives, and then move them missionally to live out the gospel in the broader community, required entrepreneurial thinking. We can learn from his organizing efforts effective ways to start new communities of faith and to reorganize current communities of faith.

Personal salvation and the broader mission of God in the world are works of the Holy Spirit. We cannot on our own "make" any of this happen. But what we can do is organize communities that are open and receptive to the work of the Spirit in their midst, both to enable us to grow in love and to give us eyes to see how God is calling persons and congregations to join in God's mission to renew all creation. Having these Christ-centered communities is our pressing need today, and the Wesleyan tradition provides the insights and guidance we need to do so.

PART ONE
COMMUNITIES
OF HOLY LOVE

1

MISSIONAL BEGINNINGS

I shall endeavor to show that Christianity is essentially a social religion;
and that to turn it into a solitary religion is indeed to destroy it.
—John Wesley, "Upon Our Lord's Sermon on the Mount" IV[1]

In 1729 John Wesley faced a choice that would profoundly affect not only his future but that of generations to come. At the time the twenty-four-year-old Wesley was serving as his father Samuel's curate, something like an associate pastor, for the parishes of Epworth and Wroot. He was also helping Samuel complete his massive *Commentary on the Book of Job*. He enjoyed the work. But John was also a Fellow at Lincoln College in Oxford University, a position that provided a more secure income than did the parish. Fellows served as mentors and tutors, each responsible for a number of students. John's absence from London had increased the workload for the other Fellows. In 1729 John was informed that if he were to continue as a Fellow, he needed to return to Oxford.

So that was his choice: to stay and help his father or to return to Oxford where his younger brother Charles attended. John decided to return. Had he not done so, I would not be writing these words, nor would you be reading this book, for Methodism as we know it would not exist. But Wesley's decision had ramifications far beyond whether or not there would be something called Methodism. It enabled him to gain a vision of transforming community that is as relevant in our day as it was for his.

The Beginnings of Methodism

By 1729 Charles Wesley had become serious about growing spiritually, much as John had done four years earlier, and had been eagerly writing his brother for advice. Both brothers sought what they called "holiness of heart and life," consisting of an intensified love for God and their neighbor. They wanted a Christ-like love that would fill their hearts, governing their desires and motivations and directing their lives. The problem was how to reach this goal.

Before John's arrival back at Oxford, Charles had already taken a step that would have immense consequences for the future Methodist movement. He had begun meeting with his friend William Morgan so they could encourage one another in practices both spiritual and academic. John would make it a threesome; then their friend Bob Kirkham became the fourth member. With John as the leader, their meetings became more regular. Insofar as this little group was known at all, it was for their devotion to receiving the Lord's Supper weekly, for which they were dubbed "Sacramentarians."

By mid-1730 Morgan was encouraging the group, now numbering six members, to visit the prisons and undertake ministries to the poor. As they began to attract more attention, they likewise attracted more derogatory names: the Bible moths (for their regular devotional reading of scripture) and the name most historians use to designate the group, the Holy Club.

In the Holy Club we already see one of the key features of Wesley's Methodism. The members followed set of rules—a "discipline"—that guided their spiritual practice daily and weekly. By agreeing to follow these rules, they committed themselves to regular prayer, fasting, the devotional reading of scripture, the Lord's Supper, and meeting together. They were also committed to a plan in which they regularly ministered to the poor and visited those in prison. Although the origin of the term is unclear, Charles Wesley believed they were called "Methodists" by others because of the methodical manner in which they went about being Christians.

In 1722 member John Clayton introduced two new features to the Holy Club that would have lasting significance. First, he encouraged participants in the Holy Club to reach out to others and for each of them to begin similar groups across the University. With a growing number of new groups sprouting up across campus, all linked to the Holy Club, their notoriety greatly increased. But this was also an early model of what later Methodism would call connectionalism.

Second, Clayton introduced the Holy Club to the writings and practices of the church of the first few centuries after the New Testament period, what the Wesley brothers would call Primitive Christianity. As the Wesleys sought to adapt these early practices (some of which, it turned out, were not as early as they then believed), they became increasingly precise about what to do and strict in doing it. They would later disavow this rigidity, but would continue to draw on Primitive Christianity as a model for the church in their own time.

What Is Methodism?

This, then, is a short account of what John Wesley in 1781 (only a decade before his death) called "The First Rise of Methodism." If you are at all familiar with John Wesley's own story, calling the Holy Club "the first rise of Methodism" may seem a little odd.

The story, as it is usually told, is that John Wesley had been seeking an assurance of salvation, which he finally found when his heart was "strangely warmed" at a prayer meeting on Aldersgate Street in London. Soon afterward he began preaching the glad tidings of salvation to large crowds in the fields. This is what is most often called the beginning of Methodism.

Yet, this conventional telling of the story is only partly correct. As we shall see, what happened on Aldersgate Street was powerfully transformative for Wesley and was a turning point in his theology and ministry. We have no desire to diminish its significance. But what the conventional story obscures is how Methodism was understood by both the Wesleys and their critics as essentially communal.

Here is John Wesley's own description of the beginnings of Methodism:

> ... the first rise of Methodism, so called, was in November, 1729, when four of us met in Oxford; the second was at Savannah, in

April, 1736, when twenty or thirty persons met at my house; the last was at London, on this day [May 1, 1738], when forty or fifty of us agreed to meet every Wednesday evening, in order to a free conversation, begun and ended with singing and prayer.[2]

This contains a second surprise for those familiar with the conventional story: he sees the *second* rise of Methodism as occurring during his time as a missionary in Georgia. Things did not go well in Georgia, in part due to John's own actions, and the result would plunge him into a spiritual crisis. Yet all did not go wrong. Looking back, Wesley sees those meetings at his home in Savannah as "the rudiments of a Methodist society."[3]

Whatever else Methodism was, for Wesley it necessarily involved persons regularly coming together to share with one another, encourage one another, and pray together. It also involved a regular pattern of prayer, scripture reading, and worship as well as reaching out to others in need.

Critics saw Methodist practices as excessive. Certainly they were not the norm for those both in and out of Wesley's Church of England denomination. For many critics all these meetings and denominational practices were unnecessary. Just attend worship, be a good citizen, assent to the teachings of the church, and you'll receive in return a happy afterlife. Why go to these extremes?

The answer is that the Wesley brothers sought a different goal than simply a happy afterlife. They did want an assurance of salvation, so it isn't as if there was no concern for their eternal destiny. But they wanted something more than this: they wanted hearts filled with and lives governed by the love of God. This was their goal, and Methodism was designed to get them there.

This goal, which they called holiness, was not understood by them as an optional extra to being a Christian. This is *God's* goal, not for a select few, but for every person. We were created in the image of God, but have fallen away. God's plan is to restore us to the image in which we were created. The brothers Wesley and their friends in the Holy Club yearned to be transformed into persons marked by Christlike love.

When someone plans a trip, it is almost always with a destination in mind. Where you are going has an impact on how you get there. One does not travel by automobile from New York to Paris—that won't get you there. Your destination also shapes your preparation. What you pack for a camping trip in the mountains is quite different for what you pack to go to the beach.

Believing that becoming persons who love as God loves was the divinely appointed goal for each human life, the Wesley brothers sought appropriate means to get them there. While there would still be more to learn, in the Holy Club they found an essential part of the answer.

John Wesley makes the connection between the goal and the Holy Club clear in recollections in a 1777 sermon. After becoming convinced in 1725, through reading several spiritual writers while a student at Oxford, that to be a true Christian is to live a holy life of love, he sought to live according to rules of discipline they advised. Speaking of himself in the third person, Wesley noted that he had sought for some that would be his companions in the way, but could find none; so that for several years he was constrained to travel alone, having no one either to guide or to help him. But in the year 1729 he found one who had the same desire. They then endeavoured to help each other, and in the close of the year were joined by two more.[4] Now having companions for the journey, they began as well to develop a regular plan of meeting. They soon agreed to spend two or three hours together every Sunday evening. Afterward they sat two evenings together, and in a while six evenings in the week; spending that time in reading the Scriptures, and provoking one another to love and good works.[5] All they were doing together was designed to enable them to journey toward the goal of perfect love.

What the Wesleys Learned

During this first rise of Methodism, the Wesleys learned four critical insights that would mark Methodism for the rest of their lives. First, the Methodist way only makes sense for persons who desire God's goals for their lives. If their lives are governed by goals of gaining wealth, fame, or success, or if it is only to obtain a happy afterlife, a community like the Holy Club makes no sense. It is a means to one end, to produce lives shaped by Christlike love.

Second, going to worship once a week, while necessary, is not sufficient to attain this goal. We need to have companions on the way. We need to be able to share with others, discuss what it means to follow Jesus in our world today, and encourage one another. While salvation is personal, it is never individualistic. To live and grow as a Christian requires community.

Third, lives of prayer, worship, and service do not happen spontaneously. We need a plan, or discipline, to organize these Christian practices so that we do them on a regular basis. Life is such that, without a plan, we become inconsistent at best. The alternative to this "Methodist" way of discipleship is all too often no discipleship at all.

Fourth, and perhaps most important, the inward transformation of hearts and lives is intrinsically linked to ministry to others. At this point Wesley and his companions are clear that a community that produces Christlike love must at the same time be a community that reaches out in love. This conviction underlay their commitment to visit the poor and those in prison. Later they would come to see that reaching out to others is itself a means through which persons are formed in love. Thus formation within the community leads to mission, and engaging in mission is itself formational.

There would be much more for the Wesleys to learn in the years ahead. In particular, they would become much clearer on the role of the Holy Spirit in both formation and mission. But what they later learned would be built upon the foundation laid in this first rise of Methodism.

Questions

Read Matthew 4:18-25

1. What similarities do you see between the missional beginnings of Methodism and the beginnings of Jesus' ministry?

2. Are there places in your local church or elsewhere where you talk with others about what it means to follow Jesus in our world today? Where are places in which those conversations might occur? What did it mean to follow Jesus?

3. Do you pray or read scripture on a regular basis? Would an agreed-upon spiritual discipline be a help to doing this, or is it not really necessary? How does Jesus' ministry affirm the goals of the Holy Club?

4. Have you ever sought to care for another person and found as a result you grew in faith, love, or understanding of God?

2   KNOWING GOD

"What then is religion?" It is happiness in God,
or in the knowledge and love of God. It is "faith working by love;"
producing "righteousness, and peace, and joy in the Holy Ghost."
—John Wesley, Letter to Mr. C—, May 2, 1786[1]

The Wesleys returned from their missionary venture in Georgia discouraged and downhearted. Charles Wesley, who had been the victim of malicious gossip as well as serious illness, returned joyously to England in 1736, but also without the assurance of salvation he had sought. John left America in late 1737 in the face of bitter opposition leading to legal action, partly due to his own rigidity in religious practice and mishandling of relationships. He had gone to Georgia in hopes of sharing the gospel with Native Americans but spent most of his time pastoring the colonists. His despair is evident in his journal: "I went to America to convert the Indians; but Oh! Who shall convert me? Who, what is he that will deliver me from this evil heart of unbelief?"[2]

But not everything went wrong in Georgia. John was especially pleased with the groups of persons he had brought together in both Savannah and Frederica for prayer, singing, and conversation—what he later called the second rise of Methodism. But he still lacked faith and with it an assurance of his salvation.

Looking back on this period in his life, Wesley would later conclude that he didn't totally lack faith. He had the "faith of a servant," a preliminary sort of faith where one knows one has fallen short of God's moral law and genuinely seeks to do better in the future. It leads to a life of dutiful obedience to God manifested in doing good works for others. The seriousness with which the Wesleys and their friends lived out this "faith of a servant" set them apart from many in the church for whom Christianity consisted of doing the minimum amount of good necessary to obtain a heavenly reward.

The faith of a servant, by showing us that we cannot earn God's favor through good works, leads us to put our trust in God rather than in ourselves. It opens us to seek and receive full Christian faith—what John Wesley calls the "faith of a child of God"—wherein we trust in what God has done for us in Jesus Christ. It is a part of our overall journey of salvation.

But this insight came later. What the Wesleys faced in 1738 was a dual spiritual crisis: lack of that full Christian faith and the accompanying assurance and lack of direction for their ministry.

The Faith They Sought

It might seem odd that two young ordained ministers like the Wesleys were seeking faith. Were they not Christians? Were they not engaged in sacrificial ministry even beyond that of a good number of clergy?

For many in John Wesley's day, faith was understood as giving one's assent to the truths of Christianity. To have faith, for example, would be to believe that Jesus is risen from the dead is as true as to believe that the earth orbits the sun. The Wesley brothers, of course, believed the teaching of scripture and the confession of the ecumenical creeds in that way. They also affirmed the doctrine of the Church of England. But this is faith understood as knowing *about* God. They wanted more than information—they wanted to *know* God in a way analogous to how we know a person.

We might infer from the created order, John Wesley later wrote, "the existence of an eternal, powerful Being that is not seen." But it is one thing to "acknowledge his being" and quite another to have an "acquaintance with him." Just "as we know there is an Emperor of China, whom yet we do not know," so acknowledging there is "a King of all the earth" is not the same as knowing that king.[3]

What clarified their need for this kind of faith was their encounter with a group of Christians from Germany called Moravian Brethren. There were Moravians on board the same ship that took the Wesleys to Georgia. When a destructive storm threatened to sink the ship, the English, including the Wesley brothers, cried out in terror. The Moravians instead calmly sang a psalm. It was clear to the Wesleys that these Christians had the assurance of salvation that they lacked.

In Savannah, the Moravian Bishop, August Spangenberg, raised questions for John Wesley about his understanding of faith and its relation to assurance. Back in London, another Moravian, Peter Böhler, showed the Wesleys that faith was trusting in Jesus Christ, and that this trust was accompanied by an assurance of salvation. Moreover, this faith was neither something to be earned or the result of one's trying harder to obtain it. It was a gift of God, received in an instant.

Once the Wesleys were convinced that this Moravian teaching was faithful to scripture, and they heard the testimonies of others who had received it, they turned to God to seek this faith. While John was the first one to become convinced, Charles was the first to have faith. Charles was ill at the time, and was being cared for at the home of John Bray. On Pentecost Sunday, May 21, 1738, while lying in bed, Charles heard a voice say, "In the Name of Jesus of Nazareth arise and believe, and thou shalt be healed of all thy infirmities." The speaker was soon identified as Mrs. Turner, the sister of John Bray, who was inspired in a dream to speak these words to Charles as the words of Christ. As a result, Charles soon found that he was "at peace with God and rejoicing in hope of Christ."[4]

While happy for his brother, this only intensified John's hunger for this same faith. It was three days later, on May 24, that this desire was finally met. Here is how John himself relates what may be the most well-known event of his life:

> In the evening I went very unwillingly to a society in Aldersgate-Street, where one was reading [Martin] Luther's preface to the Epistle to the Romans. About a quarter before nine, while he was describing the change which God works in the heart through faith in Christ, I felt my heart strangely warmed. I felt I did trust in Christ, Christ alone for salvation: And an assurance was given me that he had taken away *my* sins even *mine*, and saved *me* from the law of sin and death.[5]

Were these events the Wesleys' conversions? Charles certainly thought so. A year to the day later, he wrote the famous hymn, "O For a Thousand Tongues to Sing," giving it the subtitle, "On the Anniversary of One's Conversion." John Wesley rarely used the word "conversion," preferring instead more specific language: faith, assurance, justification, and new birth. And the more John gained clarity about the meaning of these terms, the more he found himself in conflict with the Moravians.

The Faith They Found

Let's look at these terms more closely. *Faith* is how we know God. While with "the faith of a servant" one knows and fears God, with the "faith of a child of God" one knows the love of God and trusts in the cross of Christ for forgiveness of sins. While many Moravians taught there were no degrees of faith—you either had it or you didn't—Wesley came to see that our faith can change from that of a servant to that of a child of God, and that we can grow stronger in our faith over time.

Knowing our sins are forgiven through Christ, which is *justification*, provides an *assurance* of salvation, a witness of the Holy Spirit that they are children of God. Many Moravians insisted this was a full assurance, permitting no doubt and providing continual peace and joy. Again, Wesley came to make a distinction based on his own experience and the experiences of others. We can have true confidence we are children of God, even if it is interrupted by doubt; we can have true peace and joy even if it is not constant.

Faith and justification are accompanied by a *new birth*, in which peace, joy, and love take root in our hearts and begin to grow. This new birth is the beginning of *sanctification*, a gradual growth in love and other fruits of the Spirit. The goal of sanctification was Christian perfection, the holiness John Wesley had been seeking since 1725, in which our hearts are filled with and governed by love.

Here was his most serious conflict with Moravian teaching. Many Moravians described the new birth not as the beginning of sanctification but as the fullness of sanctification. This initially confused John Wesley. He could see that there was a great transformation in his life, but he could also see that he had not reached the goal of love completely filling the heart. The new birth, he finally concluded, is not the end of the journey of holiness but the beginning.

Out of his experience at Aldersgate and struggle to properly understand it, John Wesley gained three insights that would shape his Methodist movement. The first and most important was his recognition of the power of the Holy Spirit to change human hearts. He now saw with sharp clarity that *faith*, enabling us to know and trust God, and the *new birth*, in which we begin to love as God loves, are transformative works of the Holy Spirit. This was underscored in October 1738, when he read the account by Jonathan Edwards of the "surprising work of God" that had occurred in his congregation in America. Wesley now saw the Holy Spirit as the agent of transformation, and that our becoming and growing as Christians depends first and foremost on God's grace. Our efforts do not elicit God's grace but instead are enabled and evoked by grace in the form of the power of the Spirit.

His second insight—that this is all a gift of God—led to a fundamental change in motivation. Prior to these events, John and Charles had sought to faithfully and dutifully serve God as best they knew how, fearing God's displeasure but hoping for God's approval. Now, having received faith and assurance as a gift, based not on their own efforts but on what Christ had done for them on the cross, their relationship with God changed. Instead of serving God dutifully in order to obtain an assurance, they now served God gratefully as a result of receiving assurance in Christ as a gift. Thanksgiving and love replace duty and fear as their prime motivations.

The third insight was that these motivations laid a new foundation for the pursuit of holiness. Before they tried to love God and others in hopes of pleasing God and obtaining assurance of salvation. While this genuinely propelled them into mission, it was compromised by the fact that their prime motivation was self-interest. Now they were truly set free to love as God loves, not as a means to an end, but as an end in itself. Their motivation for mission was their love for God and their neighbor.

The Wesley brothers had come to experience more deeply the meaning of 1 John 4:19: "We love because he first loved us." This verse would become a favorite of John Wesley. But they also learned that faith is necessary to our appropriating this promise, for it is by faith we know that "he first loved us."

The Means of Grace

Even before their receiving the faith of children of God and its accompanying assurance, the Wesleys had been attending the

Fetter Lane Society, a community that included both Moravians and Methodists. It was the formation of this group by John Wesley and Peter Böhler that John later called the "third rise of Methodism." Although John's questions and increasingly different understanding of faith, assurance, and new birth created some tension between the Moravians at Fetter Lane and him, these differences were not sufficient to rend the fellowship.

But that would change dramatically when Moravian Philip Henry Molther, newly arrived from Germany, "began to teach a new doctrine of 'stillness.'" Drawing on Psalm 46:10, which reads, "Be still, and know that I am God," Molther argued that in order to truly know God, one must be still; that is, cease using means of grace. Furthermore, because many at Fetter Lane did not exhibit the fullness of assurance, joy, peace, and the lack of doubt Moravian teaching said accompanies true faith, he insisted they did not have faith at all. So they should immediately refrain from means of grace and "be still."

John Wesley had been away from London, and upon returning was shocked that the stillness teaching was spreading throughout the Fetter Lane Society. The stakes couldn't have been higher for both men. Molther believed salvation itself depended on following his teaching of "stillness," and Wesley believed salvation itself was fatally compromised by Molther's new doctrine.

Wesley laid out the two contrasting views in a letter to Molther, which he reprinted in his journal. This also shows the "means of grace" at the heart of the controversy. Here is how Wesley described Molther's position:

As to the *way to faith*, you believe, that the way to attain it is to *wait* for Christ, and be *still*; that is

> Not to use (what we term) the means of grace;
> Not to go to church;
> Not to communicate [receive the Lord's Supper];
> Not to fast;
> Not to use *so much* private prayer;
> Not to read the Scripture;

(Because you believe, these are *not* "means of grace"; that is, do not ordinarily convey God's grace to unbelievers; and that it is impossible for a man to *use* them without *trusting* in them.)[6]

These means of grace Wesley will later call "works of piety," that is, they are all directly connected to our relationship with God. Molther argued that if we receive the Lord's Supper, we inevitably trust in the sacrament rather than Christ, or if we pray we trust in our prayers rather than Christ. That is, he believed means of grace inescapably led us to trust in what we do for our salvation rather than what Christ has done for us on the cross.

But these are not the only means of grace Molther questioned. Wesley listed two more:

Not to do temporal good;
Nor to attempt doing spiritual good.
(Because you believe, no fruit of the Spirit is given by those who have it not in themselves; and that those who have not faith are utterly blind, and therefore unable to guide other souls.)[7]

These means of grace Wesley will later call "works of mercy;" that is, they are focused on loving and serving others. Molther apparently believed persons who do not have the fullness of faith and salvation as he defined it could not provide spiritual guidance for others. He may also have feared that even to meet the physical needs of others would tempt us to trust in our good works rather than in Christ.

For Wesley, nothing could be more dangerous than to follow Molther's advice. As he says in his letter concerning the works of piety, "I believe, these are 'means of grace,' i.e., do ordinarily convey God's grace to unbelievers; and that it is possible for a man to *use* them, without *trusting* in them." As for works of mercy, Wesley argues that "many fruits of the Spirit are given by those who have them not in themselves; and that those who have not faith, or but in the lowest degree, may have more light from God, more wisdom for the guiding of other souls, than many that are strong in faith."[8]

We do not use means of grace, Wesley believed, because we already have all the grace we need. We use them because we are always in need of grace, and God has promised that we can come to them and find grace. And we do works of mercy not simply to receive grace but to serve God through serving our neighbor.

To put it differently, the means of grace are where God promised we would encounter the transforming power of the Holy Spirit. There we can receive faith, hope, and love, and there we can grow in faith, hope, and love. For Wesley, everyone, including seekers and other non-Christians, should use the means of grace.

John Wesley did not believe God was limited to only acting through means of grace. What he did believe is that God promised to meet us in and through means of grace.

Wesley did not just want to know *about* God but wanted to *know* God, and that we know God through faith. There is a danger of letting God as a concept replace God as a living reality in our lives. But there is another danger as well. We can take our experience of God and in a sense create the God we want. We can make God in our own image, or imagine a God that simply meets our desires or furthers our agenda.

The means of grace counter this danger because they continually bring us back to the story of God in creation and redemption, both for Israel and through Jesus Christ. Scripture and the Lord's Supper especially keep us focused on who God is, and most especially on God's love revealed in Christ. In this way we come to know God as God really is, and we in turn increasingly reflect that love as we grow in that knowledge.

The inability to bridge this fundamental disagreement led to the Wesleys and their followers to leave the Fetter Lane Society for a new society at the Foundry. The alliance between the Moravians and the Methodists was sundered.

John and Charles Wesley now were committed to those three major insights concerning how we know God. First, we know God through faith, which is a gift of the Holy Spirit. Second, this faith enables us to grow over time in the knowledge and love of God, again through the power of the Spirit. Third, the central way the Spirit works is through means of grace.

What remains is for them to link these insights with those about community and spiritual practices gained earlier from the Holy Club. It is that linkage that will put transforming community at the heart of Methodism and propel it into mission.

Questions

Read Matthew 6:1-18

1. What is the difference between knowing *about* God and *knowing* God? What difference would each make in your life?

2. How would you describe the difference between the "faith of a servant" and the "faith of a child of God?" How does the Matthew text help us to understand the difference?

3. How have you seen God at work in your own life, the life of others, or in the world?

4. What can we learn about the means of grace from the Lord's Prayer?

A PEOPLE SHAPED
FOR MISSION

What may we reasonably believe to be God's design
in raising up the Preachers called Methodists? Not to
form any new sect, but to reform the nation, particularly
the Church, and to spread scriptural holiness over the land.[1]
—*Minutes of Several Conversations Between*
Mr. Wesley and Others

This question and its answer was one of many addressed at the annual conferences John Wesley held with his leading preachers. While specifically asking about the purpose for lay preachers, the answer provides a concise summary of the mission of Methodism.

Scriptural holiness, centered on love for God and neighbor, is the mission's content and goal. The means to that goal is to reform church and society in order to return them to holiness and to spread the promise of holiness to every person in the land.

The preachers were certainly central to this mission. But back in 1738, in the aftermath of their transforming encounters with God, John and Charles Wesley knew nothing of this future mission. They were preaching justification by faith in churches, and for the most part found their message rejected and the pulpits denied to them for a return engagement. Their ministries were at an impasse.

It was a friend, George Whitefield, who opened the door to a wholly unanticipated ministry for the Wesleys. Abandoning the custom in the Church of England of only preaching in consecrated church buildings, Whitefield preached in the fields near the town of Bristol to enormous crowds. Needing to travel to Scotland and then America, Whitefield wanted John Wesley to take up the work in his stead.

Both John and Charles Wesley were wary of Whitefield's invitation. The Fetter Lane Society divided over whether John should go, until they ultimately decided by prayer and casting a lot, which indicated John should go. Thus, on March 31, 1739, John Wesley found himself in Bristol hearing Whitefield preach. "I could scarce reconcile myself at first to this *strange way* of preaching in the fields," Wesley recorded, "having been all my life (till very lately) so tenacious of every point relating to decency and order I should have thought the saving of souls *almost a sin* if it had not been done *in a church*."[2]

Two days later Wesley "submitted to 'be more vile,' and proclaimed in the highways the glad tidings of salvation, speaking from a little eminence in a ground adjoining to the city, to about three thousand people."[3] Wesley's hearers were much more receptive to his message than those in the churches. Wesley continued preaching daily and began organizing some of his respondents into groups that met weekly. By May, his brother Charles was also preaching in the fields.

Going to the People

Here was another critical lesson for the Wesleys. They would no longer wait for people to come to them but would take the good news of Jesus Christ to the people. The caring for human needs that they did in the Holy Club was now extended to encompass the sharing of the gospel itself, and reaching out to others became not just one aspect of their ministry but its central focus. Of course, at this point Methodism was not much of a movement. But that would change with two additional innovations in the 1740s that would turn Wesley's Methodism into a dynamic missional organization.

The first was the introduction of lay preachers. While initially reluctant, John Wesley became convinced after hearing one that God was indeed calling lay men to preach. More soon followed, and in time Wesley had a sizable number of lay preachers who would willingly go where they were sent. Eventually they were assigned to circuits throughout the British Isles, preaching to crowds of people with or (most often) without the permission of the parish priest.

In the 1760s Wesley began cautiously permitting lay women to preach in effect as well, just not calling it preaching. By 1771, however, he fully endorsed lay women preaching in response to a letter from Mary Bosanquet. He did not assign women to circuits, but began providing them with letters from the conference endorsing their ministries.

With this growing body of lay preachers, the missional reach of Methodism extended far beyond that of the Wesley brothers and their handful of clergy allies. But this is only the most visible part of the story. The bulk of the people called Methodists were not preachers, but they were still missional. They were also the heart of the movement.

Hearts Made for Mission

When we envision Methodists preaching in the English country-side, we likely think of them as eliciting individual conversions. This might be true for nineteenth-century revivalism in America but is misleading for Wesley's day. Those responding to the ser-mons most often were "awakened" to their sins; they had the faith of a servant but did not yet have the faith of a child of God. What they sought was the justification, assurance, and new birth the Wesley brothers had experienced in 1738. And in seeking this they did not have to struggle alone.

We opened this chapter with a question and answer from Wesley's conferences with his preachers. It was soon followed by this question: "Is it advisable for us to preach in as many places as we can, without forming any societies? The answer is short and clear: "By no means. We have made the trial in various places; and that for a considerable time. But all the seed has fallen as by the highway side. There is scarce any fruit remaining."[4]

Thus Methodist preachers always brought those who responded into community, either through forming new societies or adding them to existing societies. Wesley's account of the form-ing of the first society lays out its purpose. They met "in order to pray together, to receive the word of exhortation, and to watch over one another in love that they might help each other work out their salvation."[5] Methodists were not meant to travel the way of salvation alone. They were to journey together.

But a problem arose when the societies became too large for them to enable this to happen. The very success of Methodism in reaching large numbers of people was subverting the purpose of the societies.

From the days of the Fetter Lane Society, there had always been some Methodists who were also attending much smaller groups called bands. Borrowed from the Moravians and altered to fit with Wesley's understanding of the way of salvation, the bands were for those who had the faith of a child of God and were growing in sanctification, that is, in love for God and neighbor. The bands were confessional in nature, based on James 5:16, "Therefore confess your sins to one another, and pray for one another, that you may be healed," in this case being healed from sin (the Greek word translated "healed" can encompass both healing of sickness and salvation). The bands therefore maintained strict confidentiality given the highly personal nature of their conversations. But the bands were clearly inappropriate for the large number of the newly "awakened" who were joining the Methodist societies.

The problem was compounded in that all Methodists were supposed to follow a discipline, just as those first Methodists did in the Holy Club. In fact, to be a Methodist *was* to follow this discipline. This discipline was organized into three rules.

First, Methodists were to "do no harm." They were not to do those things that would draw them away from God or their neighbor. This would include such things as swearing (taking the Lord's name in vain), uncharitable conversation, "doing to others as we would not they should do unto us," dishonest business practices, and lives focused on acquiring and consuming (laying up treasures on earth).[6]

Second, Methodists were to do good to both the bodies and souls of their neighbors. Herein lies the foundation for Methodist mission. Doing good to bodies is a shorthand way to speak of meeting physical needs such as hunger, the need for clothing and housing, sickness, and the like. Doing good to souls is a way of speaking about sharing the gospel with others and helping others grow in their faith.

Third, Methodists were to use "the ordinances of God," that is, the means of grace. This meant attending weekly worship with a congregation as well as having a daily devotional life. It included the works of piety we discussed in chapter two: the Lord's Supper, devotional reading of scriptures, hearing sermons, prayer, fasting, and Christian conversation.

With the societies grown so large—more than one thousand members each in London and Bristol—it was hard to know if the majority of people called Methodists (those not in bands) were actually following this discipline. So even though, Wesley recalled, "we endeavored to watch over each other," there were nonetheless "disorderly walkers" in the societies. Their presence was not only scandalous but infectious, in that it could lead others astray.[7]

The solution that came was unplanned. In 1742, seeking to raise money to pay for a preaching house in Bristol, the Methodist society there decided to divide itself into classes of a dozen people each. As the leaders visited each member of their classes to ask for a contribution of a penny each, they encountered those not living in accordance with the discipline. They were in a position to personally call them to accountability. Soon classes were established in the other societies, and the practice of visiting each member was replaced by having a weekly meeting. This was the second innovation that enabled Methodism to become a missional movement.

The role of the class leader was to inquire of each member how it is with their soul; that is, where are they on the way of salvation, in order "to advise, reprove, comfort, or exhort, as the occasion may require; [and] to receive what they are willing to give toward the relief of the poor."[8] The *effect* of the weekly class meeting was to hold each member accountable for keeping the discipline.

The *impact* of the class meetings, however, would be difficult to overstate. By providing advice, encouragement, and a place for conversation regarding the discipline, Methodists were able to keep it more faithfully in the face of all the many diversions in life that work against it. This meant they were regularly practicing both works of mercy and works of piety. They were serving their neighbor as well as turning to God in worship and prayer. And as they did these things, the Holy Spirit worked in their lives to enable them to grow in the knowledge and love of God and in love for their neighbor.

No wonder Wesley could say "that the preaching like an apostle, without joining together those that are awakened and training them up in the ways of God, is only getting children for the murderer"[9] (that is, for Satan). The classes combined with the discipline were the primary means of opening Methodists to the power of the Holy Spirit. It was by way of the classes that persons came to know the love of God, transforming their hearts and lives.

They gained hearts for God, and thereby also hearts for mission to others.

Social Holiness

The term "social holiness" has in our day often been taken to mean acts of compassion and justice in society. But that was not its meaning for Wesley. He used the term to indicate Christianity is not a solitary religion but a communal one. "'Holy solitaries' is a phrase no more consistent with the gospel than holy adulterers," Wesley wrote. "The gospel of Christ knows of no religion, but social; no holiness but social holiness."[10]

This vision of social holiness—of a community of Christians who were either seeking or growing in love—was central to how Wesley understood the church itself. A faithful church was simply one in which all its members were united in the goal of being holy as God is holy, of loving as God has loved us in Jesus Christ.

The problem was that most congregations were not seeking that holiness. Wesley's hope was the Methodist movement, with its societies, classes, and bands, would be the seedbed to renew the entire church in holiness. He believed that God was doing a vast work throughout the world of which Methodism was a part, in which the entire church—Protestant, Roman Catholic, Eastern Orthodox, and Coptic—would be renewed in holiness.

We have seen how Methodist communities were designed to open persons to the work of the Holy Spirit in changing hearts and lives. What remains is to see how these communities were also centers of missional outreach. They carried out their mission in four overlapping ways.

First, they were communities of **witness**. Their very way of life together was a witness of a new possibility, a community of people whose relationships are governed by love for one another. As was the case with the first Christians, many were attracted to the Methodists because of the way in which they loved one another. It remains true today that a lot of people understand the gospel by what they see in church communities. Where there is gossip, conflict, and lack of care for one another, the gospel is discredited; where there is love for God and one another, the gospel is an embodied reality.

Second, they were communities of **testimony**. At their class meetings and quarterly love feasts, they shared with one another what God was doing in their lives. These testimonies not only encouraged others but, by hearing what God was doing in the lives of others, enabled persons to see what God was doing in their own lives. But Methodists did not keep testimony within their own meetings. They also shared what God had done and was doing in their lives with those outside of Methodism. Others were then encouraged to also turn to God through Jesus Christ. Testimonies of ordinary lay people were as critical as the sermons of the preachers in bringing the good news of Jesus Christ to the larger society.

Third, they were communities of **hospitality**. Because they sought to share good news with others and rejoiced when people responded, they were delighted to have new persons become a part of their communities. The orientation of Methodist communities was not only inward but also outward.

Fourth, they were communities of **service**. Methodists engaged in a wide range of ministries to those in need. Theirs was a world in which large numbers lived in desperate poverty, often accompanied by sickness, alcoholism, and illiteracy. Alert to opportunities to reach out in love, Methodists took initiative and organized to alleviate suffering and care for others.

In doing this they were not only living out the Methodist discipline but seeking to serve God faithfully, and those who had received the faith of a child of God were deeply motivated to love others as they had been loved by God. It was not only the Wesley brothers and their preachers who were missional but the entire Methodist movement. They were a missional people because they were a people seeking God and growing in love.

Laying Foundations for a Missional Community

What Wesley and his people did in the eighteenth century can provide guidance for us today. Leaders will not move congregations into mission by telling them that God commands it so they *"ought"* to do it. The truth is, most of us respond to such admonitions halfheartedly at best.

What is needed are people who *want* to be in mission, whose hearts are set on serving God by serving their neighbor. That happens when people encounter God's love and then love God and others in response. We come to know God's love through means of grace in transforming communities.

We can have a multitude of ways of transforming communities today. Some churches or groups may already be transforming communities without thinking of themselves as such. Others may be able to become transforming communities once they are intentional about it. In many cases there may be the need to establish new groups that can serve as transforming communities.

A number of great resources available to help persons and groups learn about community in the Wesleyan tradition. To recover the class meeting for today, two excellent resources are Kevin M. Watson's *The Class Meeting* and Steven Manskar's *Accountable Discipleship*. Both are written with local congregations in mind. Manskar's book is a more recent version of the method of accountable discipleship initially developed by David Lowes Watson for the United Methodist Board of Discipleship. His books also remain available and are well worth reading.[11]

On the spiritual disciplines, we recommend Kevin M. Watson's *A Blueprint for Discipleship*, which considers Wesley's three rules for our day in light of the challenges of contemporary culture. Bishop Reuben Job's *Three Simple Rules* is a popular book that seeks to restate the Wesley rules in a contemporary form.[12]

On the means of grace, *Eight Life-Enriching Practices for United Methodists* by Henry H. Knight III is a good introduction that takes account of today's culture. Steve Harper has written an engaging study that focuses on Wesley's own practices called *Devotional Life in the Wesleyan Tradition*. Harper has also written a book that focuses on prayer and the devotional reading of scripture entitled *Prayer and Devotional Life of United Methodists*.

And Andrew Thompson will soon publish what is bound to be a very helpful resource on means of grace.[13] Finally, on the recovery of testimony for the church today, see Henry H. Knight III and F. Douglas Powe's, *Transforming Evangelism*.[14]

These are all written for study groups in congregations as well as for personal study. Their goal is the same as Wesley's: through transforming communities to help people know God's love and then be agents of that love to the world.

Questions

1. Revivalists in the late nineteenth century spoke of coming to the altar and getting saved. Wesley's Methodists spoke of a way of salvation with conversion not as an end but the beginning of growth in love. Which of these two understandings do you think best expresses the promise of salvation in the New Testament?

2. How did Wesley's gathering people into societies and classes aid their growing in the knowledge and love of God and in love for their neighbor?

3. In what ways is your local church a witness to the good news of Jesus Christ? In what ways might it become an even stronger witness?

4. Are there opportunities to share testimonies in your church or group? What are some ways opportunities for sharing can be created?

PART TWO
COMMUNITIES
IN MISSION

4

THE WORLD
IS MY PARISH

I look upon all the world as my parish; thus far I mean, that in whatever part of it I am, I judge it meet, right, and my bounden duty to
declare unto all that are willing to hear, the glad-tidings of salvation.
This is the work which I know God has called me to: and sure I am
that his blessing attends it. Great encouragement have I therefore, to
be faithful in fulfilling the work he hath given me to do. His servant I
am, and, as such, am employed according to the plain direction of his
word, as I have opportunity, doing good unto all men. And his prov-
idence clearly concurs with his word; which has disengaged me from
all things else, that I might singularly attend on this very thing, and
go about doing good.[1]
—Wesley Journal, June 11, 1739

To this point we have described the importance of one's
heart being shaped by love in community so that one is
then ready to participate in God's transforming work of
community. While Wesley was focused internally on the heart,
as noted in the above quotation, Wesley is focused outwardly on
the implications of a changed heart. For Wesley, it is to share the
"glad-tidings of salvation."[2] The key is what he means by salvation.

It is about a new life that not only helps us to grow into the image of Christ but empowers us to see the world through God's eyes.[3]

A part of seeing the world through God's eyes is a commitment to all who are a part of our community. The idea of limiting community to only those who are a part of the congregation cheapens our love for neighbor. While helping those who are immediately a part of the congregation should not be ignored, loving our neighbor requires expanding this love to outsiders. Reclaiming Wesley's statement about the world being our parish can give us new eyes to see and experience our neighbors differently.

Community Is Our Parish

Obviously John Wesley did not say the community is our parish, but allow us to embellish for a bit. There are two key ideas that we will lift up from Wesley's journal entry about the world being our parish that translate into the community being our parish. First, we are called to the work of seeing those outside of our normal circles as a part of the community. Wesley did this personally and encouraged others to do it. For example, many are aware of the famous story of Wesley at eighty walking in the snow to collect money for the poor.[4] We do not want to simply highlight his actions but to focus on the way Wesley intentionally draws the circle wider.

One of the consistent aspects of John and Charles' ministry is that while they began with internal renewal it is always done in conjunction with an outward focus of reaching others. The Oxford Holy Club provided an opportunity for a deeper engagement of

Scripture, prayer, and so forth, but it was done with the intentional engagement of those incarcerated or disenfranchised. For the Wesley brothers, a deeper engagement of Scripture cannot be divorced from an intentional engagement with those not a part of the smaller circle.

If we think about John Wesley's word choice of "parish," then this connection becomes more interesting. The word parish is typically defined as a bounded group of individuals who belong to a particular ecclesial body. Today, Anglicans and Catholics use the term parish more than we do in Protestant circles. It would not be unusual for someone to say, "I belong to the Saint Paul parish." Meaning they attend Saint Paul for church. A parish is limited by definition because it typically refers to a particular ecclesial body.

John Wesley claims the world is his parish. In relation to the meaning of parish, it seems like an oxymoron of sorts. How can something that is limited by definition at the same time be expanded to include all of the world? Certainly Wesley had no expectation of coming into contact with every human in the world. We do not believe Wesley was suggesting this at all; yet, Wesley was committed to touching as many lives as possible with the gospel of Christ. This meant taking the gospel beyond the walls of the parish.

For Wesley the gospel was not restricted to a particular parish or confined in a building. The gospel is open to all people. "The world is my parish" is a claim that frees the gospel from the walls of the physical church. There are congregations today that perceive the walls of the building as a safeguard to keep outsiders out and insiders locked in. The good news of the gospel is confined in a box that harkens to the literal definition of parish. Wesley argued against this understanding by claiming that the world is our parish and that we are not confined in a box.

Given Wesley's broader understanding of "parish," it makes sense that we are called to both internal and external renewal. To think of one without the other is to put limits on the gospel and, dare we say, God. Throughout his life Wesley constantly expanded the circle to include those often ignored or those not in a box. This expansion is done intentionally so that those who are not currently in the box can experience the transforming power of God's grace.

In the same way that Wesley claimed the world was *his* parish, we should be claiming the community is *our* parish. It is a claim that means those not currently in our congregations can experience the transforming power of God's grace because we have not limited our understanding of community. Community is expanded to those outside the walls of our congregations.

We both have experienced numerous congregations who have restricted the circle instead of expanding it. For example, many congregations have a hard time naming five people who live within a block of the church. The assumption is that those on the block should come to the church. Wesley challenges us to go to them. In fact, we are called to *go* to them precisely because the community is our parish. Our love of God and love of neighbor are not separate acts but the same love being expressed in the way we live out being disciples for Christ. So one way for us to translate Wesley's claim that the world is our parish today is for us to expand our circles. We are called to share God's love with those beyond the walls of our buildings. In doing so we truly can claim that the community is our parish.

The second insight from Wesley that helps us to understand the community is our parish is his understanding of doing good. For those familiar with Wesley, this is not a new theme. It follows nicely from being called to expand the circle to others. A Wesleyan missional approach understands doing good not simply as gaining brownie points but as an essential part of the Christian life. Our acts of mercy toward others is a part of what it means to be a disciple. A heart rightly shaped by God's love seeks to continuously participate in acts of mercy.

We realize this idea of doing good sounds idealistic for many reasons. It is not likely that someone will do good all the time. All of us have days when we are not concerned for others and focus on our own well-being. For many of us today, we question whether our doing good is making any difference in the lives of others. For instance, we see the same faces week after week at our Saturday feeding program. While we are providing a meal for those coming, it has not made a difference in altering their weekly need for assistance.

Certainly Wesley realized that individuals do not do good all the time, and he likely experienced the constant need of helping some people time and time again. The motive, however, for helping is because of our *love* for our neighbor, not whether our actions change their lives on a permanent basis. This motive—our love for our neighbor—supersedes all the rationales we can come up with for not constantly doing good. Our doing good is not based upon outward influences but on what God has done in transforming us.

If the community is our parish, then we live out this transformation in concrete ways that God's grace shines through us. Those who are in the community experience God's grace through our loving acts. Most Christians agree on the importance of God's love and helping others in some fashion. The challenge is helping in such a way that is concrete but does not become repetitive of other social agencies.

There is a thin line between being intentional about doing acts of mercy and misconstruing these acts in terms of the church's role as a social agency. A Wesleyan missional approach seeks to do the former without getting trapped by the latter. We are called to acts of mercy bringing us in relationship with our neighbors, but these acts are possible because of God's love and transforming work in us. The acts themselves often improve one's social plight, but the church's calling is to holiness and not simply to be social caretakers. The question is, "How can we avoid erasing the thin line separating relational acts of mercy from becoming social acts of caretaking void of holiness?"

In Acts 3:1-10, Peter and John encounter a beggar in front of the Temple. The beggar in the text asks Peter and John for money. As you read this gospel story, it's easy, unfortunately, to picture the beggar being described because many of us have passed by or given money to similar individuals. In the text, Peter stops and *looks* at the beggar, and asks the beggar to *look* at him and John. This is a key part of the text that is easy to over*look*.

We can infer from the text that most people over*look* the beggar even if they help him as they enter into the temple. How many of us are like most of the people? The tendency is for us to walk by others and ignore them, or we give them a handout while we quickly continue on our way. Peter and John do something different. They stop and look at the beggar. The two of them pay attention to the beggar.

If we seek to be in relationship with those who are in the community, then we must pay attention to them. Too many congregants drive by individuals in the neighborhood, ignoring them on their way into the building. Others don't simply drive by; they often only speak or act in a perfunctory manner not requiring them to engage those in the community. In both cases those in the community are invisible to us, or we are seeing right through them. Being in relationship with someone requires us to see them and not look through them.

In his sermon, "On Visiting the Sick," Wesley states the verb "to visit" means "to look upon."[5] It is not enough to simply provide mercy from a distance. The idea of looking upon someone draws us closer to that person and into relationship with the individual. This is what Peter and John did, and it is what we are called to do in terms of doing good. By doing good in this manner, we recognize the thin line separating acts of mercy from a form of social activity void of holiness; being in relationship goes far beyond tending to social needs.

The other way that Peter and John are in relationship with the beggar, which provides a greater insight into that thin line we continue to seek to nuance, is by eliciting his participation. Peter offers his hand to the beggar and assists him in standing (v. 7). The extending of Peter's hand requires physical touch. Most likely, very few people were willing to touch the beggar. Peter is willing to do so, demonstrating to the beggar that he is not afraid of getting close to him and working with him. We need to be more like Peter, who does not simply do something to the beggar. Many of us are guilty of aiding others without really eliciting their input. We determine a community need and move forward full steam. Wesley suggests we inquire from those we are seeking to be in relationship with how we can best be of service.[6] This is another way of seeking their input and not us doing something to them. We seek to do good by participating with others and not treating others as clients.

Finally, Peter and John help us to *avoid* social activity *void* of holiness by inviting the beggar into the faith community. Verse 8 reads, "And he [beggar] entered the temple with them." Peter and John did not help the beggar and go about their merry way. The beggar stays with them. How many people have we helped and felt like we did our good deed without going any further? For Wesley doing good requires more than performing a good deed. It means taking an interest in one's spiritual and physical well-being.

As discussed above, Peter and John have already addressed the beggar's physical well-being. By staying with him and entering the Temple, they now make sure his spiritual well-being is cared for appropriately. Wesley makes clear in "On Visiting the Sick" that we are to inquire about one's physical and spiritual well-being.[7] Too many congregations focus on the physical care of others and never inquire about their spiritual needs. Other congregations focus on the spiritual needs, but never care for the physical ailments. It is not an either/or option, because doing good from a Wesleyan perspective requires both. In doing both the physical and spiritual care, we avoid engaging in social activities that mirror government or other social agencies. Our reason for doing good is based in a love for neighbor that flows from God's love for us.

We are *not*, however, advocating that congregations force individuals into the congregation in order to receive assistance. What we *are* advocating is being intentional about loving our neighbors. If we are forcing people to come to our congregation, then they are not really seeing our acts as loving. Forcing people to come for assistance typically is not effective because those being helped will see the church as a service provider and not a place for holistic healing. We must lovingly attend to their spiritual well-being as well. This is important so individuals can experience holistic healing and not simply receive the same material goods they would at a social agency. This is the Wesleyan way of doing good.

We learn from the Acts 3:1-10 story about the beggar three aspects of doing good. Paying attention to those beyond our doors; eliciting their participation in what we do in the community; and making sure we seek their physical and spiritual well-being. A Wesleyan understanding of doing good or acts of mercy include all three of these characteristics. Many congregations struggle because they do one or two of these things but not all three.

The community is our parish. By expanding the circle to move beyond our walls and by doing good we are being missional in a Wesleyan manner. When congregations are able to alter their mindset, similar to Wesley, to perceiving the community as an integral part of who they are, then those congregations begin to experience new possibilities. Being missional in the Wesleyan way will not guarantee some magical growth, but not being missional is a recipe for death. There are too many congregations on death row that have the possibility to experience new life by altering their mindset about the community.

Mission Field

Hughes Memorial United Methodist Church was started in 1949 in Washington, DC. It is a congregation that started off as a community church but over the years has seen more congregants driving in from outside of the immediate neighborhood. Hughes averages about one hundred in worship and is an older congregation. While things are holding steady right now, Hughes UMC recognizes the importance of becoming more missional.

One of the ways that Hughes UMC is seeking to make the community its parish is an effort called Community Antiviolence Program (CAP). It is a program that targets at-risk youth in the community through mentoring and tutoring. Certainly there are many congregations that have similar programs, but Hughes UMC can highlight for us concrete ways that reflect a Wesleyan missional approach for engaging the community as our parish.

It would be easy for Hughes UMC to stay completely inward focused, but they are expanding their circle by reaching out instead. Because they have expanded the circle to the youth in the community, they have been able to develop other partnerships in the community, such as providing healthy meals (through Campus Kitchen) for the youth on mentoring days. When we are willing to expand the circles, it can cause a ripple effect that puts us in contact with others we normally would not encounter.

Most of us would agree that Hughes is doing a good deed. A Wesleyan missional approach, however, is about more than simply doing good deeds in terms of being social caretakers, and Hughes is not simply a social caretaker. Hughes is intentional about paying attention to the youth who are a part of the program. They not only tutor them so that they can achieve at a higher level in school but serve as mentors so that they can be a part of their lives.

Hughes is not dictating to the community what is needed. Hughes became involved in CAP because of a partnership with Howard University that seeks to better understand the needs in the community. A part of what Hughes is trying to do is give voice to the youth. To help them to become active participants in their learning and in life. It is easy to become passive when others are always telling you what you need or what is best for you.

Everything Hughes is doing up to this point could be duplicated by a social agency. It is the last part, in conjunction with the others, that moves Hughes from social caretakers to a more missional focus. Hughes is concerned for the spiritual well-being of the students. This is shaped in a couple of concrete ways. The pastor, Paul Johnson, shares with the youth every week a single verse to help them reflect upon their week. Rev. Johnson commented, "I started off sharing an entire passage, but soon learned I was overwhelming them and moved to using one verse."[8] His goal is to help the youth to see that God is an active part of their lives by making Scripture relevant to their weekly gatherings.

Hughes also invites the youth to use their gifts in the congregation. Some of the young people are participating in a youth choir. The youth are learning songs that have meaning for their lives and spiritual well-being. It is an opportunity for Rev. Johnson and others to build deeper relationships with the youth related to spiritual issues. The youth know that those at Hughes are not only interested in their physical well-being but are concerned about their spiritual well-being as well.

Hughes is an example of a congregation that is making the community its parish. Hughes expands the circle outward as it pays attention to those often ignored. It elicits their participation and input and seeks the spiritual well-being of the youth. We can cite other examples of congregations like Hughes doing the same thing. The key is being intentional in your congregation to model a Wesleyan missional perspective. The community is your parish!

Questions

Read Matthew 6:22-23

1. What is it that we see when we look at our communities?

2. What is our motivation for doing good in the community? Do we need to work on our motivation?

3. How are we intentionally seeking to expand our circle to include others?

4. How do our ministries seek the well-being of others and share the transforming power of the gospel?

5 THOUGHTS UPON MISSION

I am not afraid that the people called Methodists should ever cease to exist either in Europe or America. But I am afraid, lest they should only exist as a dead sect, having the form of religion without the power. And this undoubtedly will be the case, unless they hold fast both the doctrine, spirit, and discipline with which they first set out.
— John Wesley, Thoughts upon Methodism, 1[1]

In recent years many individuals have commented on the famous words by Wesley in the above quote, typically arguing the current decline of Methodism in the United States and the challenges of Methodism in England are signs of "having the form of religion without the power." Certainly this observation is grounded in some truth, but it is not the entire truth. In the United States, Methodism is declining numerically and this has to be taken seriously. We believe, however, that claiming Methodism in the United States is a dead sect moves too quickly to an extreme.

The literal meaning of being dead is to have no life. While Methodism is struggling in the United States, it still has sparks of life. There are vital congregations that are big, medium, and small throughout the connection. The challenge facing Methodism today is that more congregations need to become vital. More congregations need to become missional and not simply be satisfied with existing.

Wesley penned his original letter as a warning of what could happen if Methodists became complacent with the status quo. We are playing off Wesley's original letter in this chapter by imaging a missional way forward, given the mixed bag of faith communities in Methodism today. The key for Wesley during his time was the community of faith "shedding abroad the love of God" experienced in their lives. We believe this ideal is still central today. To this end we will discuss a Wesleyan missional perspective and how it can inform our calling as congregations today. Following are our own "Thoughts Upon Mission."

Light in the Community

The image of light plays an important role in Christianity, and it is one that Wesley writes about in Sermon 24, "Upon our Lord's Sermon on the Mount, IV." The basis for this sermon is Matthew 5:13-16, which uses light as analogy for not hiding what we are doing in life, so others can see it. In part, Wesley argues that just as one would not light a candle and put it under a bushel, God has not transformed us so that we may hide it from others.[2] In fact, we would want to display the light in such a way to be a benefit to all in the house. Likewise we should openly witness about our transformation to others.[3]

If we take this analogy a step further, it helps us to understand Wesley's hope for the societies and classes. These faith communities were not to be gatherings where God's work of transformation was kept hidden, but were to be places where one witnesses to others about God's transforming power. They were to be a light to the community. There are many examples from around Wesley's time of such communities acting as a light, including this story about the "Strangers' Friends Society."

In 1791 a Strangers' Friends Society was started in Manchester, England.[4] Thomas Fildes was one of the founding members of the society, which sought to "tend to the poorest of the poor."[5] Manchester experienced explosive growth during the 1700s from about two thousand to nearly one hundred thousand people.[6] This growth created deplorable living conditions for many with some literally living below running sewage in ditches by windows they could not close.[7] The Strangers' Friends Society perceived their ministry as being a light to those individuals who found themselves in these conditions. They collected money to provide food, medicine, and clean bedding and at the same time offered spiritual assistance to those in need.[8]

Individuals like Fildes who were a part of the Strangers' Friends Society witnessed to others about God's transforming power by deed and word. This witnessing was not an attempt to make themselves seem superior to others but was an attempt to be beacons for Christ. Shining their light in this way meant moving beyond caring just for those in the Society to caring for those in the broader community. This helped to shape a Wesleyan missional approach, along with two things specific to being a light in the community that are implicit in the Strangers' Friends Society.

First, Wesley emphasized **witnessing** by deeds and words. In his sermon, "Upon our Lord's Sermon on the Mount, IV," Wesley made *clear* that the truth of the gospel has been made *clear* to us over the years by our witnessing in words and actions.[9] Those in the Strangers' Friends Society set out to address concrete issues facing the poorest of the poor. They also shared words that pointed to God's love and transforming power. The combination of these two made a powerful witness to the broader community. It is when we disconnect these two that our witness often appears dim.

The word *witness* by definition has to do with seeing. A witness is someone who sees something take place and is able to report on it. But we also judge the quality of the report. Is it accurate? Is the report of the witness clear and well presented? When we think about witnessing in this way, it is not so much of how we see, but how others see us. If others see us as dim witnesses, then it comes across like we put our light under a bushel. In our mind we may be burning bright, but others do not see our light. The way in which the Stranger's Friends Society witnessed by addressing the concrete needs of the poorest of the poor and verbally sharing God's transforming power impacted the lives of others. What made their light on the hill a good one was that others perceived their light to be burning bright as a result. Certainly they perceived the gospel from a particular point of view. It was the way in which others perceived them that made the difference in their witness.

This continues to be true. As a witness we often share from the perspective of how we see or understand things, but we must be mindful of the way others see us. Are others able to experience God's transforming love and power in the way we witness? The challenge we have today is that many do not see any light when we witness. For example, we proclaim the love of God, but the way we share makes us unlovable. While we may be speaking truth in our witnessing, are those we are witnessing to actually able to see and experience God's love? Does this mean anything goes? No. It does mean as witnesses we remember what others see in the way we share God's love with them.

Second, we are called to be authentic in what we say and do. Wesley would not use the word authentic, but we do believe he would agree with the sentiment, which is not simply saying or doing things for our own gain. Wesley used phraseology like "not desiring to honor one's self."[10] The reason we seek to be a light to the community is not so others can see us, but that they may catch a glimpse of God.

The Strangers' Friends Society did not seek to work with the poorest of the poor to make themselves look good. They did so because God was transforming their lives and they wanted to share this experience with others. They wanted to fully love their neighbors and their neighbors were not just other people in the Society. They endeavored to be authentic in their witness to those in the broader community with whom they were seeking to be in relationship.

There are several Wesleyan characteristics that inform what we call "authenticity." Authenticity from a Wesleyan missional perspective assumes intentionality about relationship-building. For Wesley it was important that we connect with the broader community. Wesley uses the language of having "intercourse with society."[11] Obviously we do not speak in the same manner as Wesley did, but one immediately grasps the meaning of his phrase.

The role of a faith community is not to be a solitary community that never builds relationships with those outside of it. In fact,

Christians need to be intentional in building relationships with those outside of the immediate community. The key is doing this authentically, in a manner that does not promote selfish interest but is focused on us becoming more like Christ. Fildes took this selflessness to the extreme by sacrificing his very life (he died of typhoid fever he contracted while visiting the sick) to help others.[12] While most of us probably will not go to the extreme of Fildes, we should take note of his commitment to visibly becoming more like Christ in the way he related to others.

The key for Wesley was that we love our neighbors because we experience God's love in our lives. We do not build relationships with others just to benefit us or our particular community. We acknowledge it is challenging to be completely selfless in building relationships with others. To a certain extent, it is impossible because we do, in fact, have a self-interest in the other person finding joy in Christ. The nuance we hope to contour is the difference between helping someone for the sole purpose of them joining our community versus helping them to experience the work God is doing in us. The former implies we are only in relationship with them because of what they can do for us. The latter means we are interested in the relationship because we have truly experienced community differently in our lives.

Individuals with whom we seek to be in relationship can quickly discern the difference. Most of us can. If we are honest, then we will admit favoring those folk we perceive as authentic and seeking to know us without strings attached. We are wary at best and often run from those who we feel are using us in some manner.

Building relationships in an authentic manner helps our lights to shine brighter.

Another characteristic of authenticity from a Wesleyan perspective is invitation. To be a light on a hill is not about one person or one community shining brightly; it is about inviting others to do so. This invitation is authentic when our lives mirror Jesus. Wesley believed that what God is doing in us is being communicated to others.[13] We are suggesting this act of communication is an invitation to others.

An example may help to make the point plainer. You love eating home-baked cakes. One of your aunts can bake the best cakes. You love going to her house because you know she will always have a freshly baked cake. One day when you go over, to your surprise, there is no cake. Another surprise, your aunt tells you she is just getting ready to bake and asks for you to keep her company in the kitchen. This happens the next few times. You start to like hanging out while she bakes and really enjoy watching the process. The next time you go over, your aunt asks if you would you like to help. You are a bit nervous but accept the invitation. It is not long before you are baking the cake yourself with her just keeping a watchful eye.

In Wesley's way of thinking, this aunt has extended an invitation to you from the moment you enjoyed eating the cakes and continuing to when you started baking them yourself. We extend an invitation to others by our deeds and words. Imagine what kind of a negative invitation we extend in partnering with those less fortunate when we make it clear we think we're doing them a favor just by being present. It will not come across as very authentic.

A part of being a light in the community is making sure the invitation we extend is one that points people to Christ and not to us or toward our particular faith community. We worship, fellowship, and are held accountable in faith communities, but ultimately our community should help people to experience the presence of Christ. This should be a part of our DNA as a Wesleyan missional community. If it is not, then we need to focus on those disciplines that can help shape us toward being more authentic in inviting others.

All faith communities are called to be a light in the community. While we used the example of the Strangers' Friends Society, witnessing to those who are wealthy is just as important. The key is not financial means but sharing God's transforming love with others. The way we witness extends an invitation to others, good or bad. An authentic invitation often makes one feel like a part of the community. An inauthentic invitation can scare someone away from joining the community. Wesley's hope was that the witness and invitation of Methodists would be a light to the world. We believe this hope is something that should still inform a Wesleyan missional approach today.

Light House

Brandon Lazarus is a student at Perkins School of Theology living in intentional community at the Dietrich Bonhoeffer House.[14] Brandon spoke at NEXT 2012 about his faith community, and one can readily see some resonances with the Strangers' Friends Society. The house is located in an impoverished area in Dallas.

Brandon starts the video by talking about how the intentional community includes those inside of the house and outside of the house.[15] The Dietrich Bonhoeffer House is a part of the Epworth Project started by Prof. Elaine Heath at Perkins, who is seeking ways to build community with the poor.[16]

The Dietrich Bonhoeffer House reinterprets the membership vows of the UMC as its way of connecting with those disenfranchised. One promises to support the faith community with prayer, presence, service, gifts, and witness (*Book of Discipline*).[17] Those in the house take these vows as a rule of life to live out in community. One of the most striking things they commit to in the house is spending four hours a week going out to be in conversation with their neighbors.[18] They are seeking to be lights for Christ in the community.

In spending four hours a week out in the community, the individuals in the house are committing to practicing witnessing, one of the key characteristics lifted up in this chapter as central to a Wesleyan missional perspective. Think about what would happen if 50 percent of the people in our congregations committed to spending one hour a week witnessing to those in the community, sharing God's transforming love with those who need to experience it.

The difference this witnessing makes is that the community begins to see those like Brandon as lights—not lights pointing to themselves but lights that point to Christ. Those in the community are witnessing the gospel in action in a different way than many have experienced in the past. All of us can be lights in the community in this way. It was folks committing to be lights for Christ that helped the Methodist movement to grow initially, and it is folks committing to be lights for Christ that can bring about its renewal.

While witnessing is an explicit part of the UMC membership vows, we believe being authentic in our engagement with others is implied in all of the vows. All that we do is a form of invitation. In the NEXT talk, Brandon discusses a young man with whom the house builds a relationship because he perceived them as authentic (our words). Authentic to the point that although they had not heard from him for a period of time, when he needed a place to go after a hospital stay, he called Brandon.[19]

The way in which Brandon had built a relationship with him made the young man feel like Brandon cared for him and did not simply see him as an object. The work of going out in the community every week and listening to their neighbors is what helps the house to build strong relationships. We can build these same relationships in our congregations and with the broader community. It means committing to going out and being with our neighbors.

The Dietrich Bonhoeffer House is just one faith community seeking to witness and be authentic its engagement with the broader community. We are going to share one more story of a very different kind of community seeking to be in community with those in the broader community.

Table Ministry

Rev. Jessica Anschutz is the lead pastor of a cooperative parish near New York City. The congregations in the parish are seeking ways to increase their vitality.[20] One of the ways they will be seeking to do so is a new effort called Table Ministry that will target young adults. Table Ministry began in the fall of 2015 with the goal of having conversations with young adults in coffee shops, restaurants, and bars.[21] The hope of these conversations is to find ways to be in community and do ministry with young adults.[22]

Table Ministry is a different form of outreach from the Strangers' Friends Society or the Dietrich Bonhoeffer House. It is a church-based ministry that seeks to address an issue facing many congregations in the United States: the need to be in community with young adults. Seeking to be in ministry this way is still about being the light of Christ. It is still about sharing the transforming power of God's love with those in the broader community.

The very nature of the ministry is set up to build relationships with young adults in the broader community. The people in the congregation will be going to the young adults' turf to hold the conversations. Anschutz believes the conversations are an opportunity for listening to and hearing young adults, and not just telling them what the congregations will be doing in regard to them.[23] Ultimately the goal is for the young adults who are interested in Table Ministry to become facilitators of groups so that it truly is a community they are helping to shape.[24] Anschutz and her team will be modeling their efforts after a Wesleyan missional approach that focuses on witnessing and authenticity.

The witness in this case is more specific because of the targeted audience. The insights from a Wesleyan missional approach are still the same. Witnessing is not simply about what those talking with the young adults know but making sure the young adults see the light of Christ shining through them. It is the willingness to meet on the young adults' turf and to listen to their stories and then not only to hear their stories but to involve them in the ongoing structure of the community. This is a powerful witness that runs counter to expecting individuals to just "fit in" to what we are already doing at our congregation. It allows for the centrality of the gospel to be maintained while being in community with those not yet being shaped by the gospel narrative.

The authenticity flows from the witness. The ministry is not a set up to simply trick young adults into joining the congregation. Table Ministry is an effort to be in authentic community with those who may not find the current faith community compelling. For Anschutz, this will not be a social club. The expectation is the small groups will reinterpret the historical Wesleyan questions as a frame for beginning the conversations.[25] For example, "How goes it with your soul?" may be restated as "How have you been challenged this week?"[26]

The point is not getting stuck on the exact wording but helping to find an authentic expression for inviting young adults to be in conversation about their souls. This is a model that other congregations can emulate—meeting young adults on their turf and being the light of Christ to them, sharing God's transforming love with the young adults and inviting them into conversations about their souls. As Table Ministry demonstrates, it is not only those who work with the poor who can be in community with others. A Wesleyan missional approach allows for all of us to find ways to be the light of Christ to others.

The question is, "Are you being the light of Christ to the broader community?" A Wesleyan missional approach offers ways for congregations to be that light in a manner that emulates practices that began around Wesley's time. It was Wesley's hope that the people called Methodists would continue to be the light of Christ to others. We believe his warning of becoming a dead sect is connected to the failure of ceasing to be this light. The good news is that we are not dead! There are those who are giving us new examples of how to be the light of Christ in the broader community. Giving us examples of how to be missional in a Wesleyan way!

Questions

Read Matthew 5:13-16

1. What does it mean to be a light in your community?

2. What is it that the community is witnessing from your congregation?

3. In what ways is your congregation's witnessing authentic? In what ways is it inauthentic?

4. What current ministry is making a difference in your community? What difference is it making in the lives of others? If you cannot name one, what ministry can you start?

6 ORGANIZING A
C.O.M.M.U.N.I.T.Y.

Lastly. As he has time, he "does good unto all men;" unto neigh-
bours and strangers, friends and enemies: And that in every possible
kind; not only to their bodies, by "feeding the hungry, clothing the
naked, visiting those that are sick or in prison;" but much more
does he labour to do good to their souls, as of the ability which God
giveth; to awaken those that sleep in death; to bring those who
are awakened to the atoning blood, that, "being justified by faith,
they may have peace with God;" and to provoke those who have
peace with God to abound more in love and in good works. And
he is willing to "spend and be spent herein," even "to be offered
up on the sacrifice and service of their faith," so they may "all
come unto the measure of the stature of the fulness of Christ."[1]

My brother Wesley acted wisely. The souls that were awakened under his ministry he joined to societies, and thus
preserved the fruit of his labor. This I neglected, and my
people are a rope of sand.[2] (George Whitefield)

One of the reasons Methodism continues today is John
Wesley was a great organizer of missional communities.
This ability to organize communities is at the heart of
what made Methodism thrive during Wesley's day and is essential

to renewal in our own day. It is not enough to simply be a community manager. Whether starting a new church or renewing an existing congregation, leaders must be able to organize communities in such a way that their members are growing in spiritual depth while being outwardly focused.

The Wesleys spent their lives committed to helping others grow in spirituality while being in mission to their neighbors. As indicated by the quote above, this was and should be the character of a Methodist. It is not simply an emphasis on these two ideals that have sustained Methodism since the 1700s but the ability to organize faith communities that enacted these ideals by keeping them at their center. George Whitefield, a contemporary of the Wesleys, did not have the same lasting legacy as the Wesleys, because he was not as successful in organizing such communities.

Whitefield was a great preacher, but his impact, by his own account, was greatly lessened because those he touched could more easily fall away. Whitefield begins the quote by saying, "My brother Wesley acted wisely." It is our hope that we will heed Whitefield's words and act wisely today. We will once again emphasize organizing communities so that the people will not be like a "rope of sand." In this chapter we will offer insights into what it means to be an organizer and discuss some of the characteristics that inform a Wesleyan missional approach to it.

Organizer

One of the challenges in today's culture is often the words "organizer" or "community organizer" are associated with political interest. If we take a step back and consider the root meaning of organizing, then it helps us to broaden our understanding of this term. An organizer is someone who can put things together for a common purpose. For example, a closet organizer enables one to put all of their dress clothes in one space, casual clothes in another, and shoes in some orderly fashion. Whereas all of these items may have been mixed up and all over the place in the closet, a closet organizer brings them together in a way that fits their common purpose.

Someone who organizes communities brings people together for a common purpose. If we live in a neighborhood where cars go speeding by daily and we fear for our children playing outside near the street, then someone who brings us together to advocate for speed bumps is an organizer. In the same way the Wesleys were organizers. John and Charles brought people together to work out their salvation. This common purpose informed the reason they organized individuals into societies, classes, and bands. They did not bring people together for the purpose of "church growth." The fact that the societies, classes, and bands fueled the growth of the Methodist movement is a byproduct of the common purpose for which they organized people.

John Wesley writes, "This was the rise of the **United Society**, first in London, and then in **other places**. Such a society is no other than *a company of men having the form and seeking the power of godliness, united in order to pray together, to receive the word of exhortation, and to watch over one another in love, that they may help each other to work out their salvation*"[3] [emphasis mine]. The Wesleys were clear on the common purpose of the societies. The desire to work out one's salvation and do so through works of piety and mercy flowed from this understanding. For the Wesleys, the daily activity of being a Methodist meant loving God and neighbor, which was a living out of the common purpose for which the societies existed. The Wesleys left the Fetter Lane Society and started the Foundry Society, because their understanding of the common purpose for transforming community was centered in works of piety and mercy.

A part of the genius of the Wesleys was sustaining this common purpose in the community. It is one thing to organize for a common purpose that is short term and will end but another to organize around an ongoing work that is for a lifetime. Wesleyan communities were designed for lifelong participation. As Christians we never stop loving God and our neighbor. This common purpose that unites us is a lifetime commitment.

While we could lift up many things that informed the way the Wesleys organized communities, three we just highlighted are 1) a defined common purpose; 2) living out the purpose daily; and 3) recognizing it is a lifetime work. How do these three inform our work in faith communities today? A challenge today is too many congregations do not know the common purpose that unites them or they unite for the wrong purpose. Individuals often join congregations because that is where their friends attend or it offers social visibility. What we do not hear is the explicit use of Wesleyan language naming the common purpose as one seeking to work out one's salvation, or to grow in the knowledge and love of God and neighbor. We do not hear a commitment to growing in spiritual depth while being missionally focused.

Admittedly this challenge is different for a congregation that has been around for one hundred years versus a new church start. The older congregation may have had a common purpose initially, but at this point no one recalls it. A part of renewal is to help the congregation to organize around a common purpose. We, of course, believe focusing on love of God and neighbor is still a vital purpose today. For new church starts, it is important to be clear about the common purpose when the community is started. Vital faith communities are clear about their common purpose and all of their activities flow from this purpose. In part we believe this is why the Wesleys were so successful.

Yet having a common purpose is not enough. Living out that purpose daily is necessary. We live in a society captivated by metrics. We are not going to rehash the pros and cons of measurements. One of the insights from a Wesleyan missional perspective is we should be committed to works of piety and mercy every day. If we are committed to these practices daily, then we will experience transformation. The metrics of loving God and neighbor are what we are called to daily as Christians. Are we faithful in prayer, reading Scripture, and visiting the disenfranchised? This seems simple and straightforward, but if we are honest, many of us fail miserably at loving God and our neighbors daily.

In fact we often spend more time on building maintenance and figuring out how to survive. We are consumed with the wrong things. The Wesleys did not set out to create thousand-member societies. They organized small groups of individuals committed to the daily work of loving God and neighbor. We also should be consumed with loving God and our neighbors as we seek to transform faith communities today.

That the work of loving God and our neighbors will never end is a challenge. It is easy for prayer, taking Communion, or even visiting the disenfranchised to become rote over time. We continue to do these things, but they are no longer transforming because we do them out of mere duty. Loving God and neighbor cannot be done out of duty; it has to be a part of what it means for us to be in a faith community. A community structured in such a manner may at times grow weary, but at its core still experiences the joy of a heart filled with God's love and sharing this love with its neighbors. It is this work that sustains long-term the community and does not detract from its purpose.

The Wesleys were organizers of communities and this is the work we are called to today. What are some of the characteristics that help to facilitate transformation? As we explore the acronym C.O.M.M.U.N.I.T.Y., we will highlight these characteristics in light of a Wesleyan missional perspective.

C.O.M.M.U.N.I.T.Y.

CONNECT

The Wesleys were great organizers of community, but what are some of the characteristics that helped them to shape the community toward a common purpose, a purpose lived out daily, one that is ongoing? The first characteristic of community is *connect*. The Wesleys were able to connect individuals together in various ways to live out works of piety and mercy. Their ability to connect individuals together started with them connecting themselves to other like-minded people in the Oxford Holy Club.

The work of connecting individuals around the work of holiness continued their entire lives. Individuals came together for prayer, Scripture, and Communion. These same individuals connected with others in the broader community to make a difference in the lives of others. At the heart of holiness is connecting to God, to others in the faith community, and then to others in the broader community. All of these connections are important and essential for a Wesleyan missional effort.

The tendency for too many congregations today is to connect with one another and then to choose either connecting with God *or* with those in the broader community. This is not usually a conscious choice. But to focus on spiritual growth while not reaching out to the broader community compromises that growth. We cannot grow in love if we are not acting in love to others both in and outside the community. The focus on service without a relationship with God is to ignore the very source that enables us to love and do so in a way that respects the dignity of others. The Wesleys always connected in all three ways because all three work together for what it means to fully love God, self, and neighbor.

In our efforts to organize communities today, we must be mindful of connecting in all three ways or we will continue to struggle. God transforms us in community so that we can participate in the transformation of the broader community. This means actively connecting with others to make a difference in their lives and not being satisfied with maintaining the status quo of our faith community.

OPEN

Changing the status quo in a community is challenging. This means the community has to be *open* to all and actively seeking others. The Wesleys were able to accomplish this by making sure the societies were open to all, but as one continued on the journey of salvation they also provided the opportunity to be with a smaller group of people who wanted increased commitment and greater accountability.

The fact that the community was always open to new individuals starting the journey meant not staying static. It is easy to become comfortable with the status quo of one's community. There is something reassuring about seeing the same familiar faces week after week that provides stability in life. The way in which the Wesleys organized a community provided stability in a different manner. The stability comes from the common purpose for which the community exists. It does not matter if people come or go, because everyone is committed to the practice of loving God and neighbor.

We recognize that most faith communities today will nod in agreement. The challenge comes when they look hard in the mirror and see some of the barriers to entry that they are unconsciously promoting. For example, some congregations without saying a word promote "paying your dues" to be in leadership. All of the folks in leadership have served at the church for over twenty years so I know, as new person in the community, I probably cannot hold a leadership position. This is just one example, but the key is looking in the mirror and being honest about your barriers to entry.

The United Methodist Church, like most mainline denominations, is fascinated with growth right now. One of the precursors to growth is an openness to others. The Wesleys organized communities in such a way that they encouraged them to always be open to others participating. New church starts and church renewals have to encourage an openness to others, or they will ultimately maintain the current status quo. That status quo leads to decline!

MERCY

A Wesleyan understanding of community is shaped by *mercy*—the mercy we receive from God that helps to shape our lives toward deeper piety and the mercy we are to extend to others so that they also can experience God's grace. It is important that we remember it is because of God's mercy that we can fully experience God's love. For all of us the fact that God unconditionally forgives is hard to comprehend. It is when we start to actively receive God's mercy through worship, prayer, and other means that our lives are transformed.

When our lives are transformed we seek to be in community in a different way with others so that they also can experience this transformation. In chapter four, we referenced the Strangers' Friends Society and the work they were doing to broaden community. This work was possible because they had experienced God's transforming work in their lives and sought to share it with others. The transformation of community is not possible without God's mercy and the sharing of God's mercy.

We live in a world where showing mercy is at times perceived as a weakness. For example, we teach children in sports to exploit the weakness of your opponent. A Wesleyan perspective runs counter to this ideal because it is not about exploiting the weakness of your opponent. It is about extending grace where your opponent is weak and helping them to transform the weakness as God has done to us. Certainly the analogy does not work completely, because in sports one is trying to win, but in life, winning should not be at the expense of another. A community shaped by mercy is a community where lives are changed because acceptance of all is more important than the victory of a few.

MUTUALITY

It is sometimes easier to respect someone who is similar to you than someone who is different. During the Wesleys' time, the disenfranchised were often overlooked by those with some economic means. The disenfranchised are still often overlooked today. The idea of a mutuality between those with means and those without runs counter to the way many of us experience community. The norm is that those with means have their communities and those without means have their communities. They are rarely in community with one another.

The expectation is that those with economic means have something to give to those disenfranchised while the disenfranchised do not have anything to give. A transformed community means developing a different understanding of mutuality where all individuals are respected equally, and all have something to give to the community. While giving includes meeting economic needs, it encompasses so much more. The ability to really experience this sort of give-and-take requires a different mindset in the way we interact with one another.

One of the reasons that the Wesleyan classes worked was because of a certain degree of mutuality. Everyone truly sensed an accountability to others in the group regardless of social status. The mindset was not that "because of my position in society I only have to answer questions from those with a similar position." This high level of mutuality requires a certain vulnerability that makes many of us uncomfortable.

Starting or sustaining a community where individuals practice mutuality toward one another is a challenge. When the community loses this practice it is even harder to recover it. This is one of the reasons that reclaiming the common purpose of the community is critical. To put it in Wesleyan language, focusing on working out one's salvation and developing ways to support each other in that work can help to restore mutuality. We understand this is not an easy task, but if we truly are seeking community, it is a necessary task. Mutuality is often ignored, but should be at the heart of what it means to be in community.

UNCONVENTIONAL

John Wesley is remembered for many things, but one of them is his preaching in the fields. Field preaching was not the conventional way during his time. In fact, John was skeptical of this practice at first. He bought into this unconventional practice because it gave him a way of reaching more people to experience the transformation of Christian community. Today we often herald what Wesley did and seek to emulate it in some way. We think that if we can just find that one thing, like field preaching, everything will change.

We misunderstand Wesley's example if we think there is some magic thing that will solve all our problems. We may spend all of our time focusing on the magic and not doing the work of practicing transformation. However, we do need to be more intentional about being creative in our context. Wesley preaching in the fields was unconventional, but it worked in his context. We have to find those things that can be just as transforming in our contexts.

What works in Oklahoma may not be the same thing that works in New York. Our ability to really understand the contexts in which we work helps us to be creative as we broaden and sustain community. For example, individuals making personal house calls may be perceived as hospitality in one neighborhood but quite the opposite in another. Understanding context can help us to develop creative ideas for connecting with others. When we make these connections, we have to make sure the individuals begin to learn about the common purpose of the community and the daily practices sustaining it. Too often we become enamored with what we are doing and forget that the real reason we did something unconventional in the first place was to continue the work of transforming community. A Wesleyan missional approach calls for us to be unconventional in connecting with others, but doing so as a means of furthering the work of community.

NARRATIVE

We often use the term narrative today in the same way that some talked about the "old, old story." The narrative is the way we inhabit the biblical text. For the Wesleys, the narrative shapes us toward a deeper love of God and neighbor. When we are inviting and sustaining people into and in the community, it is the narrative that enables us to have common language to make this happen. Simply put, the community shares a common narrative.

One of the compelling things about the biblical narrative is it allows for people to enter into the narrative at different points in time. It should not be dependent on one person to keep the community going. It is the biblical narrative, not the pastor or leader, which is the source of community life. We all have access to the narrative and through it are able to invite and sustain others in the community.

Many of us have watched the original *Law & Order* television show. If you can remember when the show started in 1990, then you also know that the main characters at that time are very different than those appearing on the show in later years. It is one of the few shows that changed main characters over time without a negative impact on the show. The narrative of the show was so compelling that it allowed for various people to come in and fill a role on the show. We believe the biblical narrative is far more compelling than any television show and allows for all of us to be involved in inviting and sustaining others in community. The narrative is not dependent on one person.

We have to make sure in our faith communities that all of us have a stake in the narrative. It is not enough for a few to know the narrative. In chapter two we talked about knowing God. In part, we know God because of the narrative. We are able to share the narrative so others also may know God. At the heart of what the Wesleys did in transforming community was keeping the narrative at the forefront of the community.

INVITATIONAL

The word *invite* in a Christian culture is not as straight forward as it seems. We typically think of an invite as asking someone to come to something and that is the end. When we extend an invitation, we give individuals information pertaining to some event and once we do, our job is finished. When we do invite people to a church event, the people in our congregations operate in this same manner as those in general. We give out information about an event and that is it for us.

In Christianity, and certainly for the Wesleys, invitation has an aspect that goes beyond the simple sharing of information. The challenge is to make an invitation to a transformed life in a community that will help you to live it out. At one level, Christians are extending an invitation to others to come to something, but the something is not a one-time event. The something is a transformed life lived in a particular community for the rest of one's days.

At the heart of this invitation is the same invitation that Jesus extended to the disciples. The disciples were invited to experience God's transformation lived out in community with Jesus and each other. The Wesleys followed this model in the way they invited others to experience God in the societies, classes, and bands. We are called to model this invitation in the way we invite others into community. This means our invitations must be more than asking persons to attend an event. Our initial contact with persons may well be through their coming to events, but our hope should be for all to experience God's transformation in a community.

Trustworthy

One of the challenges any community faces today is trust. For those outside of the community and even for some insiders, the question is, "How do we know we can trust you?" There are various reasons that individuals do not trust faith communities. It is important for communities today to be as authentic as possible. When we are authentic, people are more likely to trust us.

Many of us have experienced the difference between someone who is trying to get our business at all cost rather than the person who genuinely is trying to help us. The person trying to get our business at all costs comes across as inauthentic, because we do not really believe what the individual is saying. They may say they are trying to provide something beneficial to us, but we suspect that is not their true motive. Someone who has our genuine interest at heart comes across very differently.

Unfortunately, in the church we often come across as the first and not the second. The Wesleys were authentic in connecting with others, because they genuinely cared for their souls and physical needs. They did so in such a way that people felt they genuinely cared about them as people. Today, people are more wary of individuals who say they are interested in their souls, but really are not genuinely concerned about their well-being. We have to find ways to reach out to others that come across as authentic and not inauthentic. Being trustworthy will help a community to invite and sustain others on the journey.

Yearning

The word yearning is another way to describe our ultimate hope. The Wesleys' yearning was for transformation into the image of

Christ. This yearning led them to be in community throughout their lives seeking this transformation by daily practice of love for God and neighbor. The question is, "What is our yearning today?" Is it to be transformed into the likeness of Christ? Or is it to be a place where people come to help us celebrate another congregational anniversary?

There is nothing wrong with celebrating congregational anniversaries, but when that becomes what defines us as a congregation, we are yearning after the wrong thing. The emphasis should not be on making it another year and being satisfied that we are more than one hundred years old. The emphasis should be on holiness and being restored into the image of Christ. It is this yearning that is enduring and interprets the narrative in a way in which all can participate.

Unfortunately we are drawn away from this yearning when we start focusing on surviving. We start thinking about what we cannot do or what little we can accomplish instead of continuing to live out the daily work of loving God and neighbor. When a congregation declines, it often starts to yearn for the days when it was once vital. That yearning needs to be turned toward that which can make it vital again: a Wesleyan missional approach focuses on yearning for transformed hearts that enable us to daily love God and neighbor. It does not settle for anything less.

Conclusion

These nine characteristics help us to better understand a Wesleyan missional approach for transforming community. We are not suggesting that every congregation will exhibit every characteristic or exhibit it to the same degree, but we do believe congregations need to pay attention to these characteristics. For example, Hughes UMC, which we discussed in chapter 4, is doing a great job of connecting and being unconventional. This does not mean it is ignoring the other letters in the acronym, but these two characteristics are more prominent at this time. Jessica Anschutz's Table Ministry in New York, while also focusing on connecting, is being intentional about mutuality and trustworthiness.

The point is, while we naturally emphasize different characteristics depending on where we are on our journey, we should always be trying to engage all nine in some manner. The Wesleys successfully organized their communities around these characteristics. We believe congregations can find ways to do so today, not simply for the purpose of adding people to the roll but for greater discipleship.

Some of you are thinking this sounds great, but how do we get started in making this transformation? There is no one way to do anything. We suggest taking honest inventory of what is the common purpose of your faith community and how is it lived out daily. Transformation is never easy, but it is immensely satisfying when it deepens our relationship with God and enables us to bring others into a loving community.

Questions

Read Matthew 7:24-29

1. On what foundation are we building our community?

2. What are the characteristics of the acronym that best support the foundation of our faith community today? What characteristics do we need to work on to create a stronger faith community?

3. Are there ways in which our congregation is like a rope of sand? What can we do to address this concern?

4. What new missional effort can your congregation start that will make a difference in people's lives?

NOTES

CHAPTER 1

1. John Wesley, "Upon Our Lord's Sermon on the Mount, IV," par. I.1. *Works* 1:533.

2. John Wesley, "A Short History of the People Called Methodists," par. 9. *Works* (Jackson edition) 13:307.

3. John Wesley, "On Laying the Foundation of the New Chapel," par. I.4. *Works* 3:582.

4. Ibid. Par. I.1. *Works* 3:581.

5. Ibid.

CHAPTER 2

1. John Wesley, Letter to Mr. C—, May 2, 1786. *Works* (Jackson Edition) 13:132.

2. John Wesley, Journal, January 24, 1738. *Works* 18:211.

3. John Wesley, "Original Sin" par. II.3. *Works* 2:177.

4. Charles Wesley, Journal, May 21, 1738. St. Kimbrough and Kenneth G. C. Newport, eds., *The Manuscript Journal of the Reverend Charles Wesley, M. A.* (Nashville: Abingdon Press, 2008), 1:106–8.

5. John Wesley, Journal, May 24, 1738. *Works* 18:249–250.

6. John Wesley, Journal, December 31, 1739. *Works* 19:132.

7. Ibid.

8. Ibid., 133.

CHAPTER 3

1. "Minutes of Several Conversations between Mr. Wesley and Others," *Works* (Jackson edition) 8:299.

2. John Wesley, Journal, March 29, 1739. *Works* 19:46.

3. Ibid., April 2, 1739.

4. "Minutes of Several Conversations between Mr. Wesley and Others," *Works* (Jackson edition) 8:300.

5. John Wesley, "A Plain Account of the People Called Methodists," I.7. *Works* 9:255–256.

6. John Wesley, "General Rules of the United Societies" 4. *Works* 9:70–71.

7. John Wesley, "A Plain Account of the People Called Methodists," II.1–2. *Works* 9:260.

8. Ibid., II.5. *Works* 9:261.

9. John Wesley, *Journal*, August 25, 1763. *Works* 21:424.

10. John Wesley, Preface to *Hymns and Sacred Poems* (1739), 5. *Works* (Jackson edition) 14:321.

11. Kevin M. Watson, *The Class Meeting* (Wilmore, KY: Seedbed, 2013); Steven W. Manskar, *Accountable Discipleship* (Nashville: Discipleship Resources, 2003). David Lowes Watson's books were originally published by Discipleship Resources and are now reprinted by Wipf and Stock. They include *Accountable Discipleship, Covenant Discipleship, Forming Christian Disciples,* and *The Class Leader.*

12. Kevin M. Watson, *A Blueprint for Discipleship* (Nashville: Discipleship Resources, 2009); Rueben Job, *Three Simple Rules* (Nashville: Abingdon Press, 2007).

13. Henry H. Knight III, *Eight Life-Enriching Practices of United Methodists* (Nashville: Abingdon Press, 2001); Steve Harper,

Devotional Life in the Wesleyan Tradition (Nashville: Abingdon Press, 1983) [There is also a workbook edition of this book published by Discipleship Resources]; Steve Harper, *Prayer and Devotional Life of United Methodists* (Nashville: Abingdon Press, 1999). Andrew Thompson's new book is scheduled for publication by Seedbed.

14. Henry H. Knight III and F. Douglas Powe, Jr., *Transforming Evangelism* (Nashville: Discipleship Resources, 2006).

CHAPTER 4

1. John Wesley, *Journal, Works* 19:67.

2. Ibid.

3. Henry H. Knight III and F. Douglas Powe, Jr., *Transforming Evangelism: The Wesleyan Way of Sharing Faith* (Nashville, Discipleship Resources, 2006), 16.

4. John Wesley, *Journal*, January 4, 1785, *Works* 23:340.

5. John Wesley, "On Visiting the Sick," par. I.2. *Works.*

6. Ibid., par. II.2.

7. Ibid., par. II.4.

8. Paul Johnson, Interview by F. Douglas Powe Jr., Mount Vernon Place UMC , 6.17.15.

CHAPTER 5

1. John Wesley, "Thoughts Upon Methodism," *Works* 9:527.

2. John Wesley, "Upon Our Lord's Sermon on the Mount, IV," para. II.5. *Works.*

3. Ibid.

4. Steve Rankin, "The People Called Methodists," in *From Aldersgate to Azusa Street: Wesleyan, Holiness, and Pentecostal Visions of*

the New Creation, ed. Henry H. Knight III (Eugene: Pickwick Publications, 2010), 40.

5. Rankin, *The People Called Methodists*, 41.

6. Ibid.

7. Ibid.

8. Ibid.

9. Wesley, "Upon Our Lord's Sermon on the Mount, IV," para. II.6.

10. Wesley, para. IV.2.

11. Wesley, para. I.2.

12. Rankin, "The People Called Methodists," in footnote 14, 42.

13. Wesley, "Upon on Our Lord's Sermon, IV," para. I.7.

14. Brandon Lazarus, "Brandon's Talk at NEXT," Vimeo video, 13:33, posted by United Methodist Collegiate Ministry, 2012, accessed on August 3, 2015, https://vimeo.com/53879409.

15. Ibid.

16. Elaine A. Heath is the McCreless Professor of Evangelism at Perkins School of Theology in Dallas, Texas.

17. *The Book of Discipline of the United Methodist Church 2012*, ed. Neil Alexander, (Nashville: The United Methodist Publishing House 2012), ¶217, page 153.

18. Brandon Lazarus, 2012.

19. Ibid.

20. Jessica Anschutz, "Leading Congregational Outreach and Growth in a Pluralistic Culture: Final Assignment," (Term paper, Wesley Theological Seminary, 2015), 1.

21. Ibid.

22. Anschutz, 2.

23. Ibid.

24. Ibid.

25. Anschutz, 8.

26. Anschutz, 8—9.

Chapter 6

1. John Wesley, "The Character of a Methodist," *Works* 9:41.

2. Adam Clarke, *The Life of the Rev. Adam Clarke*, Book 3, Chapter 2.

3. John Wesley, "The Nature, Design and General Rules of Our United Societies," *Works* 9:69.

CPSIA information can be obtained
at www.ICGtesting.com
Printed in the USA
BVHW04s0254231018
530961BV00006B/60/P

9 780881 777543